ROBBY

Written and illustrated by K G Subramanyan

Seagull Books
CALCUTTA, 2019

First published in 1972 at the Fine Arts Fair
by the Graphic Art Department,
Faculty of Fine Arts, M. S. University of Baroda.

Seagull Books, 2008
Second printing, 2019

ISBN 978 8 1704 6 288 0

Published by Naveen Kishore
Seagull Books Private Limited
36C, S.P. Mukherjee Road, Calcutta 700 025

Typeset by Seagull Books, Calcutta, India
Printed and bound by Hyam Enterprises, Calcutta, India

May be
they named me Robby.

But Pa calls me
Baba
Ma calls me
Dumpling
Sis calls me
Booby
And Aunt calls me
Silly

But
I can be more still

Like the ant
in the anthill

Like the bird
in the birdcage

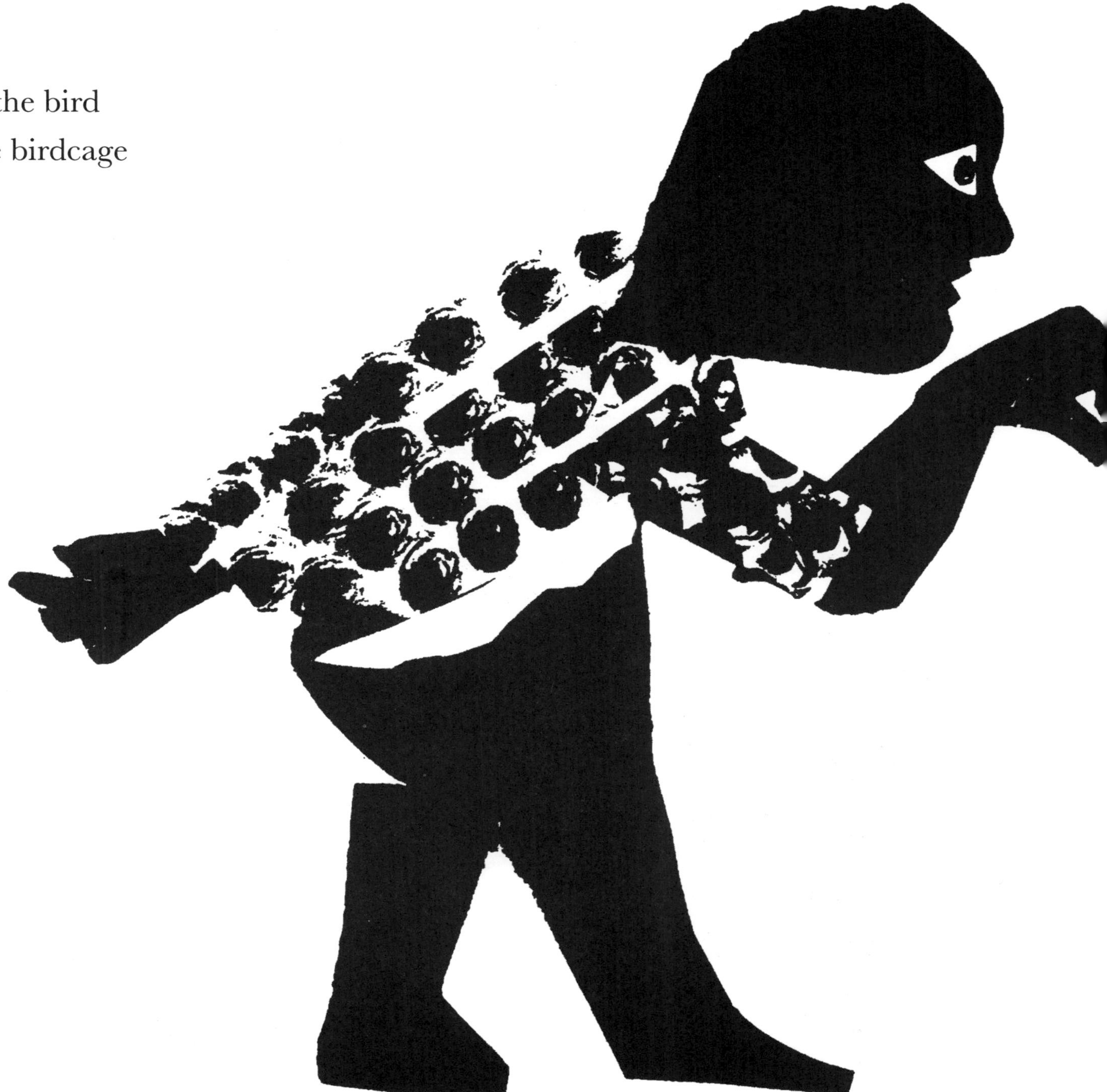

a funny little
bunny

or jolly little
polly

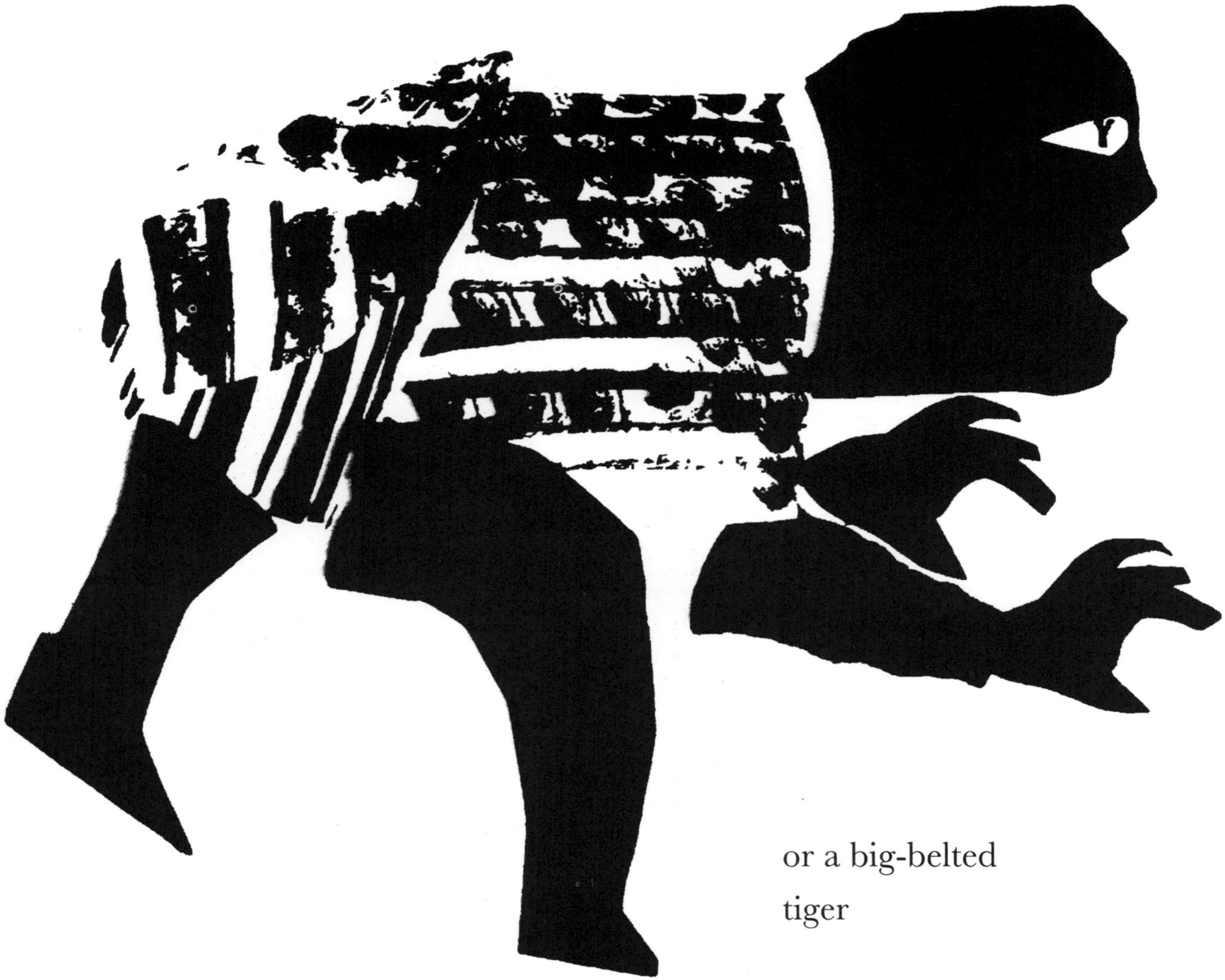

or a big-belted
tiger

or a spot-quilted
leopard

or a rip-roaring
lion

or a gut-goring
bison

or a but-butting

billy

or a strut-strutting
peacock

Spiky-spoky
hedgehog

Gawky-walky
camel

Do you think
it is funny
For one to be
So many?

May be
they named me
Robby.
But Pa calls me Baba
Ma calls me Dumpling
Sis calls me Booby
And Aunt calls me Silly
But I can be more still
Like the ant in the anthill
Like the bird in the birdcage
a funny little bunny
or jolly little polly
or a big-belted tiger
or a spot-quilted leopard
or a rip-roaring lion
or a gut-goring bison
or a but-butting billy
or a strut-strutting peacock
Spiky-spoky hedgehog
Gawky-walky camel
Do you think it is funny
For one to be so many?